I0417703

TABLE OF CONTENTS

Be a Prepper – Survive Any Disaster or Crisis

Prepare for the Worst; Hope for the Best
©2013 by Dr. Harry Jay

DISCLAIMER AND TERMS OF USE AGREEMENT:

(Please Read This Before Using This Book)

This information is for educational and informational purposes only. The content is not intended to be a substitute for any professional advice, diagnosis, or treatment.

The authors and publisher of this book and the accompanying materials have used their best efforts in preparing this book.

The authors and publisher make no representation or warranties with respect to the accuracy, applicability, fitness, or completeness of the contents of this book. The information contained in this book is strictly for educational purposes. Therefore, if you wish to apply

Introduction

"No man who is not willing to help himself has any right to apply to his friends, or to the gods."

Demosthenes (384–322 BC, Greek statesman and orator of ancient Athens)

Welcome to SurvivalNations' "Be A Prepper" Program. We are glad to have you with us! Becoming a "Prepper" isn't what most people think it is. We are not a group of survivalists waiting for the end of the world, Armageddon, or 2012. We do not preach doom and gloom messages nor are we out to scare the living daylights out of anybody.

Actually, we are very much pessimists by trade and optimists by nature. We see world events just like you do but we see them as an indicator and not as fatalists.

We subscribe to the philosophy that becoming prepared is just plain smart. We operate from the premise that in any disaster or crisis, the government will not be able to help us; that all services will be cut off and that we must take care of ourselves, our friends, family and neighbors by banding together "in numbers" or as we call them "PrepperNations" so that we can pool our resources, our talents, and most importantly - our faith for the common good.

We accomplish our goals by networking with like-minded people such as yourself that want to be prepared – but prepared properly – and that have a desire to meet like-minded people because there is strength in numbers.

You will meet fantastic people through "Be a Prepper;" ones that have a heart to help and teach. Sharing knowledge and resources and assisting people in time of need is almost built into their DNA.

Everyone comes from different walks of life; some have much and many have little. By banding together, the strong can help the weak and encourage one another when disaster or crisis strikes.

So have a little fun, meet some nice people and gain some knowledge that will help you in the future.

Once you become a "Prepper" you can help spread the word and get the ball rolling in your area.

You too can form or become a member of a PrepperNation and feel good about yourself. It's all about people helping people and in time of need we really do need each other.

We ARE NOT all in this together ALONE but we are a group of PrepperNations and we ARE prepared!

Chapter 1 - Prepper Meet-Ups called PrepperNations

Members of PrepperNations are called "Preppers" and they become member of local PrepperNation groups to share resources, learn survival techniques, socialize, etc.

To find a group nearest you write to: mailto:support@epubwealth.com.

If there is no group nearest you then you can form your own PrepperNations group in your area.

Resources

Go here and download your free survival planning guide: http://bit.ly/pFfYG0
Go here and download the "Be A Prepper Kit":

http://www.filefactory.com/f/c254b26d637a9514

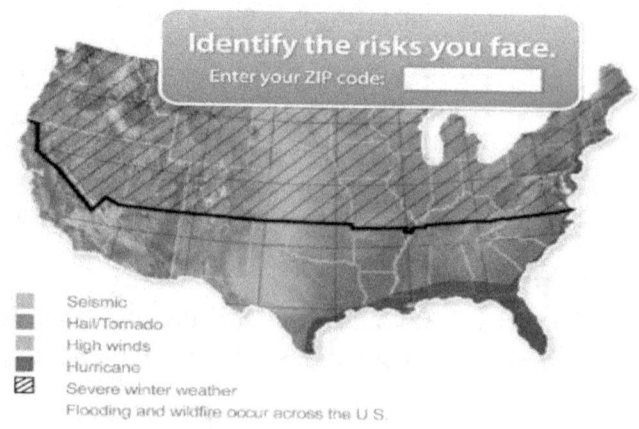

http://www.disastersafety.org/

Depending on where you live, the risk factors you face from natural disasters are different. Go to the website listed above and plugin your zip code to see what your risk factors are.

Discussion Topics:

You must always be prepared to evacuate immediately.

If the police came to your door and said you have 30-minutes to evacuate, would you be ready? Here is what I've done to be prepared for whatever might happen.

- I have taken my personal identification items such as:
    - Drivers license
    - Birth certificate
    - Passport
    - Credit cards
    - Bank records
    - Financial records
    - Easy-to-carry mementos like my marriage license, some of the kids school drawings and photos
    - All of our jewelry, etc.
    - Medical – all prescriptions and shot records

I placed them in expandable plastic folders that you can get at any office supply. Do not use paper expandable files (they fall apart easily); buy plastic ones (I bought a half dozen in different colors). I also bought a barrel bag and placed all of my folders in the bag ready to grab it and go.

- I also placed in my new barrel bag
  - A couple of day's food supply
  - Energy bars
  - Trail mix
  - Sunflower seeds
  - Some water packets (do not use bottled water in your evacuation kits. It is heavy and takes up too much room. Use water packets)
  - Water purification pills
  - A flashlight
  - A radio
  - Batteries
  - A cell phone charger
  - Pens and pads of paper
  - Extra pair of glasses (if you wear them or contact lenses)
  - A first aid kit with plenty of Band-Aids of all sizes
  - Toilet paper (and feminine napkins)

- High potency multi-vitamins
- Disposable razors
- Personal grooming kit for nails
- Toothbrushes
- Deodorant
- Bar soap
- Wash cloth
- Hand towel
- 5-day change of underwear, socks, t-shirts
- A jogging suit
- New tennis shoes
- A poncho (can double as a shelter)
- A new (in the pack) air mattress
- A lightweight windbreaker.

I know it seems like a lot but actually you can get a ton of stuff in a barrel bag especially if the stuff is new and has never been unpacked from the original packaging.

You must also consider a partial loss of services versus a total loss of services or a complete breakdown of the social infrastructure.

I always plan for the worse so here is the checklist to consider and you can add to your "stash" as you go along or do it all at once.

It took me 9-months to assemble mine so start with the **"emergency evacuation kit"** first and then work up to the **"remain in your home kit"**

I accumulating all of my stuff from the manufacturers I have listed below and got my family involved when I decided on the right mix.

My daughters have their own stash and their food selections are different due to taste differences. Get your family involved in all of your preparations.

It is a good time to discuss procedures, where to find out emergency information during a crisis, a central meet-up location or back up if all transportation comes to a halt.

This isn't easy during a crisis because many if not all services are shut down.

Phone service will most likely be interrupted but not the internet.

Note: Regular land line and cell phone service most likely won't work depending on the type and severity of the crisis. If you can afford it, I recommend a satellite phone. I use mine when I travel overseas all of the time but they are not cheap. But then again they work all of the time too. Here is the one I have and I love it - http://bit.ly/nof138.

Mine has all the bells and whistles and you don't need this so just buy the basic version for $799. Also, AT&T is the carrier and check with them for the prices of their service plans before you buy. This phone works EVERYWHERE but is more expensive to use than a cell phone so don't think you can get one of these in lieu of your cell phone.

Make sure everyone knows where to post that they are all right and their location like a central Facebook page.

As you become prepared, they too will see the value. Fear is a conscious mind reaction to being without control.

Becoming prepared and getting family involved really cuts down on the fear factor.

I even got my whole neighborhood involved and held a block party to discuss it with my neighbors. This is how PrepperNations was born! It really pulled my neighbors closer together and now I live in the best prepared neighborhood on the planet.

We even appointed a crisis team that will go house-to-house to check on everybody to see if everyone is okay.

Neighbors can share equipment, supplies and assist one another especially if some are injured. There IS strength in numbers, people!

Okay, let's continue...the following is not based on immediate evacuation (that was covered above) but being able to stay in your home without services available. Storage will become a main issue and I placed all of my stash in plastic storage bins that you can get at Wal-Mart. They cost $49 and have wheels (very important because mine weighs a ton)

This makes them vermin proof and easily stackable and away from moisture. Be sure to label each bin with what is in it.

Chapter 2 - Survival Checklist

Everything listed below is represented in the product section

1. **First Aid** – Do NOT buy a skimpy first aid kit; invest a little more and buy the best!!! In the products section of this report I offer products I have used and found that they deliver what they say and what I need. I also added to my first aid kit the following: hydrocortisone crème, anti-bacterial crème, anti-fungal cream, an antihistamine and saline spray, aloe vera lotion, rubbing alcohol, sewing kit, extra bandages, and last (don't laugh) a fifth of Jack Daniels in a plastic jug (do not have anything breakable in your stash). If you or your family is diabetic, make sure you have plenty of insulin and the paraphernalia that goes along with it like a testing meter (don't forget batteries), etc. Pay extra attention to any and all medications and prescription drugs you and your family is taking. Assume you will not access to prescription drugs! Remember, your "stash" is what is going to keep you and your family alive so give this a very critical eye and thought!

2. **Records** – personal as well as family identification items, i.e. drivers license, birth certificate, passport, credit cards, bank records, financial and investment records, easy-to-carry mementos like your marriage license, school

records, real estate deeds, inventory of household goods for insurance purposes (also take photos of the inside of your home) and all insurance records including property and casualty and life and health insurance.

3. **Keepsakes/Valuables** – this is a tough one because you must remember that most likely you will be carrying this stuff with you so I recommend photos and jewelry and/or anything light and valuable (don't even think of taking your shotgun collection – lol).

4. **Children Needs** – for babies I recommend you buy the inflatable "water wings". You can use these to place on either side of a baby to keep it from moving or rolling around in its sleep. Keep a separate barrel bag for kids and mostly put in it clothes, some lightweight toys, any medication, personal stuff like glasses, dental retainers, etc.

5. **Elderly Needs** – Medications and keeping warm are the two primary considerations to elderly care. Be sure you have a good supply of hearing aid batteries, back up glasses, dentures, etc. Extra air mattresses are a good idea too.

6. **Pet Needs** – always have a portable transportation kennel on hand if you need to take your pet with you. Even if "Rover" is well trained and stays with you, a situation may occur with other animals around where you will need to place your pet in its kennel for its own protection. Also leashes and even a muzzle should be in your kit. Always have at least a month's supply of pet food on hand and any medication your pet is taking.

Grooming aids are important but only a couple items are necessary like a brush or comb.

7. **Food/Seeds** – This is the most important. Having a supply of stored food and seeds in case of an interruption in the food supply cannot be emphasized enough. I have given some extensive coverage to food products in the product section below because of its importance. I always have at least 12-months food supply in storage (my stash) but depending on the size of your family, you may want to increase or decrease this. The food products come in their own storage containers and can be stored up to 25-years. Cooking without access to a stove is also covered in the products section.

8. **Water** – Water is a must (use pouched and not bottled because it is lighter and easier to carry) but more important is having a water purification system in order to make your own water supply. This is the one I use at home: http://bit.ly/qSZz7w. Technology is such that there is now available atmospheric water makers that actually makes water from air. Since all survival food is freeze-dried, water is the most important aspect of survival. Besides using it for food preparation, you will need it for drinking and bathing. More on this later...

9. **Fuel/Power** – There are different types of fuel to consider. If you have a power generator, for example, either gasoline or diesel needs to be stored. Don't forget that your automobile has fuel in the gas tank. You also need fuel for cooking

14

and possibly staying warm. I discuss in detail alternative energy supplies like wind and solar. All of this is covered in the product section. Care must be given in storing flammable liquids. Go here to learn how: http://bit.ly/rcZC9r

10. **Hygiene/Sanitation** – VERY IMPORTANT! A good many diseases can ensue quickly if sanitation is overlooked and sewage is not disposed of properly. One thing I added to my stash was a medical book. The primary goal is to stay as clean as possible even if taking a "sponge bath" is all that is available. More later on this...

11. **Lights & Radios** – always purchase a light that has a hand-crank in lieu of a battery-operated one. I actually have both. My light also has a radio built into it but the quality is not the best. I will show you where to buy the best radio in the products section. You will need to be able to keep in touch with local authorities in order to keep up to date with what is happening and what services are provided locally such as FEMA updates, etc. Get a good radio! Solar-charged lights are also best and there are even solar-charged lanterns available.

12. **Tools** – you will want a toolkit that can be rolled up with a tie string to take with you. Do not get a kit with a hard case. You only want the essentials – hammer, pliers, saw, etc. I also placed some steel stakes for my shelter and some flares in my toolkit.

13. **Shelter** – I use my poncho to double as a tent. If you buy a tent, get one with the floor built-in or a

one-piece tent so it keeps out the dirt and moisture (rain). Make sure it is lightweight. I bought a small pup-tent but it is light and easy to carry and completely made out of nylon.

14. **Transportation** – I went and bought a bicycle and an electric scooter. Don't bother with buying a gas-powered scooter. If gas is available then you can use it for fuel.

15. **Weapons** – I also placed a hunting knife and pistol in my stash. If everything breaks down and goes chaotic, you will most likely need to defend yourself and your family. Don't forget ammo too.

16. **Entertainment** - When you think of survival preparation usually the last thing you think about, if you think about it all, is entertainment. But how do you keep the kids busy? And how do you keep family members focused on positive things rather than depressive things? And don't forget yourself; you too need to keep a positive mindset.

This is what I have done: First I loaded up my laptop with movies. You can easily get tons of movies and music here for only $24.95 per year: http://www.vuze.com/.

Next, I bought a Kindle ebook reader for $139 or you can buy a used one for about $90: http://bit.ly/mZtK4s. You don't need the one with all the bells and whistles just the basic one like I got.

Go online to find ebooks, comics, novels, newspapers, movies and more for my ebook reader. Actually there are things here for the whole family. I use this site: http://epubwealth.com.

Go online here: http://www.wilderness-survival.net/ for an incredible FREE survival guide. Honestly, I cannot believe it is free. Don't think because it is so comprehensive that it includes survival in just about any and all situations that it doesn't apply to you. Read it! Study it! It will assist you in formulating your plan and make you aware of things you may not have thought about in your planning stages.

Emergency Evacuation Kits – I have purchased every one of the evacuation kits below simply to try them and test them. I have provided different ones based on price and quality. They are all good but differ in what they carry and the amount they provide so click on each link and check them out carefully based on your needs. These are important! If you have to run quickly this is what you will survive on so don't skimp and remember to buy based on how many people these kits will support!!!!

Chapter 3 – Emergency Survival Products

I have tested and tried almost every manufacturer and products listed here so you can be assured you are getting the best. Note: At all times I have attempted to take into consideration cost and price but candidly, if it tastes like the inside of your boots, I don't care how inexpensive it is; I didn't list it but I have listed what I feel is the best product at the best price. Everyone's budget is different so concentrate on your emergency evacuation kit first and then schedule out a plan to acquire everything you need over a period of time. NOTE: if some of the links are broken just write to me: support@neternatives.com and I will replace them for you. I can't list all the companies I use otherwise this report would begin to look like a small novel (lol).

Amazon has some nifty survival products in general at some great prices too. I buy a good amount of food here plus I really like their food bars. Also, they have an emergency backpack at a price I haven't been able to beat. Click here and check them out: http://amzn.to/qxOZfo

EcoloBlue is the coolest and latest technology for water. It makes water from air, which means it pulls the water vapor from the air and filters it before dispensing it. My unit makes 30-liters of water per day. Check it out: http://bit.ly/nzJgNH

QuakeKare is where I get all of my water products including my water purification tablets. You must have these and a water filter too. Also be sure to click on the sanitation link. Very important! I buy all my sanitation products here. Check it out here: http://bit.ly/qvnSMO

1-800-Prepare.com is where I get the majority of my survival stuff. On the Home Page, just look at the menu bar on the left. They have excellent pet survival kits too. They have a huge selection and pretty good prices. Go here: http://bit.ly/oVSyoi

This is where I get my tents. I especially like their "modular tents. They are all one piece with the floor attached, which is important. Look at the top of the Home Page in the upper left menu bar for "Modular Tent System". They have good all around prices and great customer service. Go here: http://bit.ly/qaJb7r

This site has really good clothing and I have even purchased some knives here too. A bought a good deal of clothing here. Go check it out: http://bit.ly/q1XdXV

Two things here: 1) Supplies for the elderly and; 2) they have an inexpensive First Aid kit. Check out the side menu bar and go here: http://bit.ly/nsHvuJ

Are You Prepared is one of my main survival sites and one of my favorites. It is packed with free information and really good stuff. Allow yourself at least 30-minutes to browse this site. It is really worth your time. Go here: http://bit.ly/pnrqxa

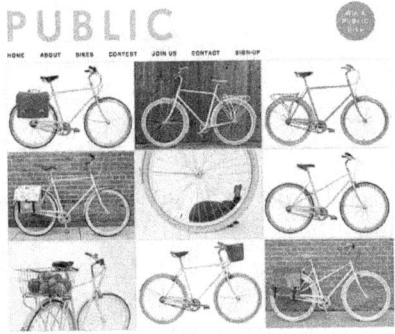

I purchased my bike here because a friend of mine has a Public bike and it is built to last. These bikes do not break. It reminds growing up when I had a Schwinn bike. Both are solid, dependable and tough…good bike to have in a crisis. Cool colors too; go here: http://bit.ly/r0bwCY

I bought my Ezip 500 Electric Scooter and I love it except it only goes about 8-miles before I need to recharge it but for an emergency it is perfect. When I was researching getting an electric moped, I wasn't looking for speed or looks. I did want more range but this bike is so easy to operate and so reliable, I can live with the range issue. Go here and check out the different models: http://bit.ly/qygSoq

I really like this site for the best prices, and delivery. They have sales quite often and notify me by email of their sales. I can't complain about their quality and their food is some of the best I have tasted. Try them: http://bit.ly/oLy9p0

C.CRANE

CC Crane has the finest radios - emergency as well as non-emergency. I own two of them plus a half dozen of the L.E.D lanterns which have hand cranks on them. I also have a couple of handheld two way radios. You cannot beat the prices or quality of CC crane. http://bit.ly/qHwueK

New Survival Seed Bank Lets You Plant Full Acre Crisis Garden!

One of my most favorite sites is called "Solutions in Science". Go here and check it out: http://bit.ly/p5bGg5. They have top quality survival stuff that I have found is fantastic. Everything I have purchased from their site is rugged and works better than what they said so go check them out. They have solar power generators (I bought mine here and survival seeds (I bought mine and just for fun planted some and you will not believe the produce I got.). Everything dealing in survival is on this site so plan some time to peruse it.

I looked high and low for a generator that was portable and easy to use. I love my solar power generator. Actually I wasted my money buying a gas-powered generator. Be careful to match up the correct generator with your needs. I wanted one that would run my laptop so check the "specs" on each one. Go here: http://bit.ly/qHFoe3

Being a naturally curious sort of dude, I asked my doctor and dentist what people did in the old days before modern medicine. What if they had a toothache or abscess? What about painkillers? I have to tell you, I was amazed at the answers I received. When drugs weren't available or even invented yet, they used herbs and natural cures or candidly, they simply died. I did some research and found this guidebook on how to make my own herbal medicines and after reading it and trying it, I make some pretty good stuff. I actually prefer using my own home-grown remedies rather than store bought so by this; it is worth its weight in gold. Go here: http://bit.ly/r8Vhoy

I am one person and my kids are grown and gone so in my plan, I only need to provide for myself. This crisis cooker is the keenest thing I have found and it is so easy to use and clean. If you have a big family then you will need a bigger unit but I would get one of these as backup. Go here: http://bit.ly/pTxIEf

The Importance of Non-Hybrid Seeds - Non-Hybrid or Open-Pollinated seeds allow the gardener to collect seeds from a crop for future planting. Hybrid seeds do not. All Heirloom Organics Seed Packs are 100% Non-Hybrid AND Non-GMO (genetically modified) and **specially sealed for long term storage**. Use now AND save for emergency. All from the same hermetically sealed pack! And non-hybrid seeds do not cost any more than hybrid seeds! Go here: http://bit.ly/r7l0HE

This is where I buy my weapons and I buy a good many guns mostly as a hobby and collector. Their prices even

beat gun shows…yes they are that good. Be sure to check with your local authorities if you plan on carrying your weapon concealed. The laws are different in all states and localities regarding concealed weapons. Please stay legal! Also, whatever you decide on buying, please be sure you qualify on it by going to a shooting range and getting proper instruction. http://bit.ly/p5CCn3

Oh yeah, do not forget ammo too! http://bit.ly/nsovlH

Also, checkout Brownell's Sinclair International division; they have good stuff too. http://bit.ly/pXBsEq

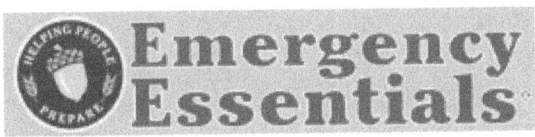

Here is a great site for bulk purchases for those with big families or particular items you need individually. Candidly, Emergency Essentials is good for anything in the survival category. I buy a good deal from this site so check it out carefully. They have one of the biggest inventories of all my suppliers. http://bit.ly/q2qKMX

I Have a Special Gift for My Readers

I appreciate my readers for without them I am just another author attempting to make a difference. If my book has made a favorable impression please leave me an honest review.   Thank you in advance for you participation.

My readers and I have in common a passion for the written word as well as the desire to learn and grow from books.

My special offer to you is a massive ebook library that I have compiled over the years. It contains hundreds of fiction and non-fiction ebooks in Adobe Acrobat PDF format as well as the Greek classics and old literary classics too.

In fact, this library is so massive to completely download the entire library will require over 5 GBs open on your desktop.

Use the link below and scan all of the ebooks in the library. You can select the ebooks you want individually or download the entire library.

The link below does not expire after a given time period so you are free to return for more books rather than clog your desktop. And feel free to give the link to your friends who enjoy reading too.

I thank you for reading my book and hope if you are pleased that you will leave me an honest review so that I can improve my work and or write books that appeal to your interests.

Okay, here is the link…

http://tinyurl.com/special-readers-promo

PS: If you wish to reach me personally for any reason you may simply write to mailto:support@epubwealth.com.

I answer all of my emails so rest assured I will respond.

Meet the Author

Dr. Harry Jay is Director of Research for AppliedMindSciences.com, a mental health and mind research group of Applied Web Info, and is the author of over 100 books and research papers as a behavioral scientist.

In his 32-year career, Dr. Harry Jay has contributed many new mental health treatment treatments and protocols using some of the new advances he has discovered in Energy Psychology.

He specializes in addictions of all kinds, sexual abuse, child predation and gender relationships.

He is also a board member to ePubWealth.com and serves on the science committee assisting non-fiction science writers in book publishing and promotion.

As a leading behavioral scientist, he provides profiling services to the company's ForensicsNation.com unit as well as criminal psychology research to aid in identifying and apprehending child predators and cyber-criminals of all kinds.

He resides in Southern Utah and enjoys the outdoors, fishing and photography.

Visit some of his websites

http://www.AddMeInNow.com
http://www.AppliedMindSciences.com
http://www.AppliedWebInfo.com
http://www.BookbuilderPLUS.com
http://www.BookJumping.com
http://www.EmailNations.com
http://www.EmbarrassingProblemsFix.com
http://www.ePubWealth.com
http://www.ForensicsNation.com
http://www.ForensicsNationStore.com
http://www.FreebiesNation.com
http://www.HealthFitnessWellnessNation.com
http://www.Neternatives.com
http://www.PrivacyNations.com
http://www.RetireWithoutMoney.org
http://www.SurvivalNations.com
http://www.TheBentonKitchen.com
http://www.Theolegions.org
http://www.VideoBookbuilder.com